PAINTS PLUS

Gillian Souter

Gareth Stevens Publishing
A WORLD ALMANAC EDUCATION GROUP COMPANY

★ Before You Start ★

Some of these projects can get messy, so make sure your work area is covered with newspaper. For projects that need paint, you can use acrylic paint, poster paint, or any other kind of paint that is labeled nontoxic. Ask an adult to help you find paints that are safe to use. You will also need an adult's help to make some of the projects, especially for cutting with a craft knife.

Please visit our web site at: www.garethstevens.com
For a free color catalog describing Gareth Stevens' list of high-quality books and multimedia programs, call 1-800-542-2595 (USA) or 1-800-461-9120 (Canada). Gareth Stevens Publishing's Fax: (414) 332-3567.

Souter, Gillian
    Paints Plus / by Gillian Souter
      p. cm. -- (Handy crafts)
    Includes bibliographical references and index.
    ISBN 0-8368-2821-6 (lib. bdg.)
    1. Painting--Juvenile literature. 2. Handicraft--Juvenile literature.
  [1. Painting. 2. Handicraft.] I. Title II. Series.
  TT385 .S685   2001
  745.7'23--dc21   00-052243

This edition first published in 2001 by
Gareth Stevens Publishing
A World Almanac Education Group Company
330 West Olive Street, Suite 100
Milwaukee, Wisconsin 53212 USA

This U.S. edition © 2001 by Gareth Stevens, Inc. Original edition published as *Art Works* in 1999 by Off the Shelf Publishing, 32 Thomas Street, Lewisham NSW 2049, Australia. Projects, text, and layout © 1999 by Off the Shelf Publishing. Additional end matter © 2001 by Gareth Stevens, Inc.

Illustrations: Clare Watson
Photographs: Andre Martin
Cover design: Joel Bucaro
Gareth Stevens editor: Monica Rausch

Printed in the United States of America

1 2 3 4 5 6 7 8 9 05 04 03 02 01

Contents

Ready, Set, Paint!

**You will need some tools
and materials before
you begin painting.**

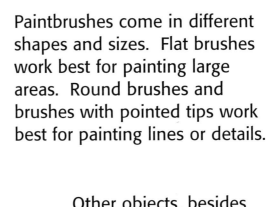

Paintbrushes come in different shapes and sizes. Flat brushes work best for painting large areas. Round brushes and brushes with pointed tips work best for painting lines or details.

Other objects, besides brushes, can be used to apply paint, too. An old toothbrush is good for spattering paint. A cotton swab can be used to paint details. A sponge will not leave brush marks.

You can use more than just paint to create art. Some projects in this book use other materials, such as paper, to add color.

Always use paints that are nontoxic and water-based. These paints include poster paints, which come in bottles or blocks, and acrylic paints, which are sold in tubes. If a project list includes paint, either of these types can be used safely.

Remember to put the lids back on paint containers, or the paints will dry out.

Paste paint is ideal for finger painting or for creating artwork that needs a thick, slow-drying paint. To make paste paint, mix equal amounts of flour and water, then add paint to color the mixture.

Color Chaos

You need only red, yellow, blue, black, and white paints to create all the colors you want.

Mix colors to make more colors.

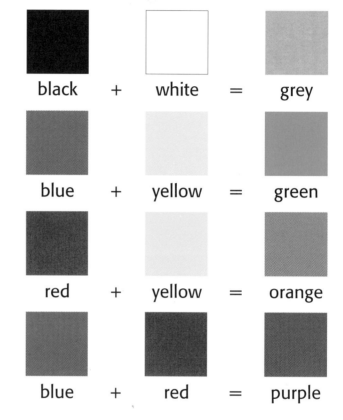

black + white = grey

blue + yellow = green

red + yellow = orange

blue + red = purple

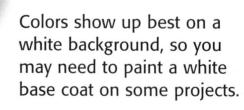

Colors show up best on a white background, so you may need to paint a white base coat on some projects.

6

If you add white paint to a color, you make a paler shade of that color.

A plastic lid makes an excellent palette for mixing paints.

You can make acrylic and poster paints thinner by adding water to them.

Always cover your entire work area with newspaper. Keep a large jar of water handy for rinsing brushes before you change colors of paint.

When you finish painting, carefully clean your brushes in soapy water.

Sponge Surprise

Believe it or not, a simple sponge is all you need to paint a pretty speckled pattern.

You Will Need
- tin can
- acrylic paints
- flat paintbrush
- sponge
- scrap paper
- clear varnish

1 Make sure the tin can is clean and dry and has no sharp edges. Paint the outside of the can with two coats of white paint.

2 Carefully tear off the edges of a sponge. Taking off the edges keeps lines from appearing as you paint.

3   Dip the sponge in red paint, or some other bright color, and dab the paint onto scrap paper. Keep dabbing it until you like the pattern it makes. Then dab the sponge lightly around the sides of the can.

4   Also use the sponge to wipe paint around the rims at the top and bottom of the can. When the paint on the can is dry, brush on a coat of varnish.

★ Bright Idea ★
Your cleverly speckled
container makes a handy
holder for pencils –
or paintbrushes!

Totally Tartan

Bonnie plaid book covers will give your school books Scottish style.

You Will Need
- flat paintbrush
- white paper
- poster paints
- round paintbrush
- book
- scissors
- removable tape

1 Use a flat paintbrush to cover an entire sheet of white paper with a pale-colored poster paint.

2 When this base color is dry, use the flat brush, again, to paint wide stripes across the paper with a different color of paint.

3 Later, use a round brush to make stripes that run up and down in a third color. Let the paint dry.

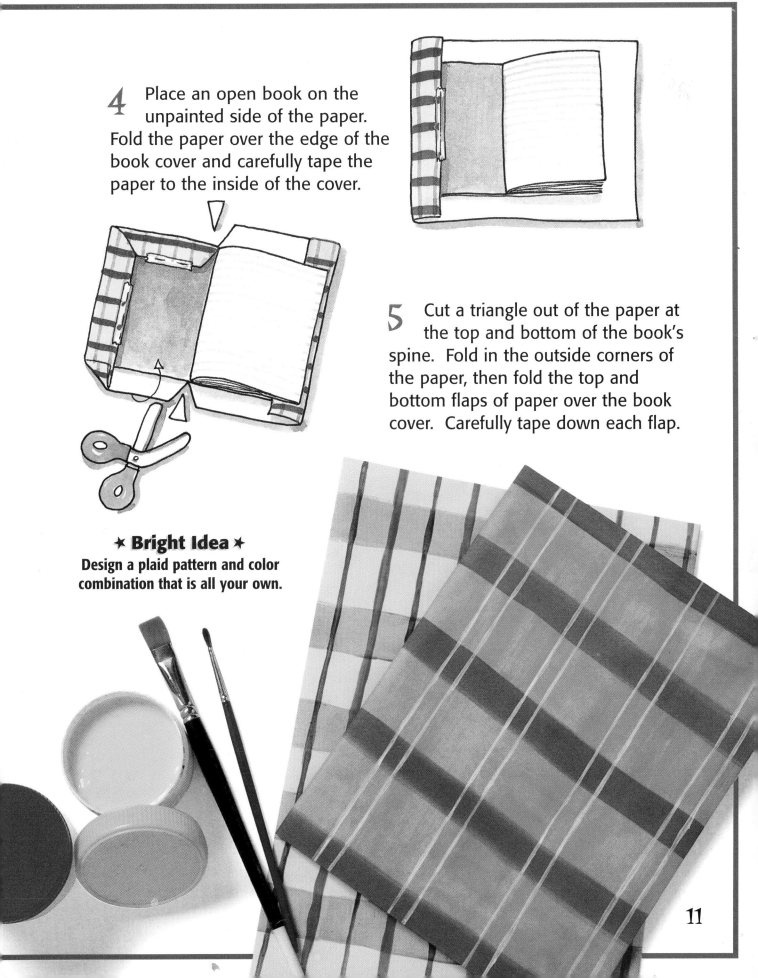

4 Place an open book on the unpainted side of the paper. Fold the paper over the edge of the book cover and carefully tape the paper to the inside of the cover.

5 Cut a triangle out of the paper at the top and bottom of the book's spine. Fold in the outside corners of the paper, then fold the top and bottom flaps of paper over the book cover. Carefully tape down each flap.

★ **Bright Idea** ★

Design a plaid pattern and color combination that is all your own.

Zing the String

Painting crazy, curly designs can be easy. All you have to do is pull a few strings.

You Will Need

• scissors
• plastic sheet
• pillowcase
• fabric paints
• small bowls
• string
• book

1 Cut a sheet of plastic to fit inside a pillowcase. Place the plastic inside the pillowcase to keep the paint from soaking through.

2 Pour each color of fabric paint into a small bowl. Dip pieces of string into the paint. Make sure the strings are coated well.

3 Lay each painted string in a loose coil on one half of the pillowcase, keeping one end of each string at the edge.

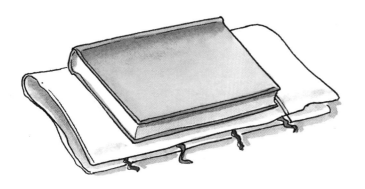

4 Fold the other half of the pillowcase over the strings. Lay a book on top of it to add weight.

5 Pressing down on the folded edge of the pillowcase with one hand, pull the strings out, one at a time, with the other hand. Unfold the pillowcase and let the paint dry. Check the instructions on the paint to find out how to make it permanent.

★ **Bright Idea** ★
Paint your pillowcase in colors that match your bedroom.

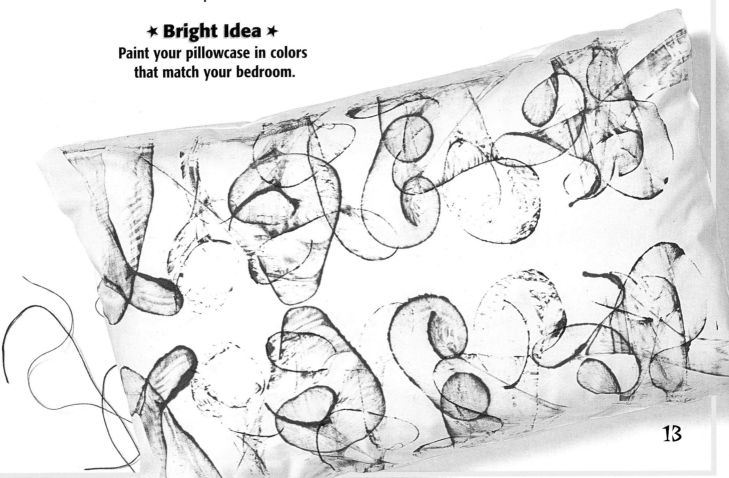

Spatter Attack

When you want to be cool, spatter some paint on paper, then fold the paper into this fancy fan.

1 Cover your work area with newspaper — spattering is very messy! Then paint a large sheet of white paper with a base color.

2 Let the base color dry. Add water to a second color of paint to make it thinner. Dip a toothbrush into the paint. Spatter the paint onto the paper by pulling your finger across the toothbrush.

3 For bigger spatters, dip a round paintbrush into the paint and flick it at the paper. Let the paint dry.

14

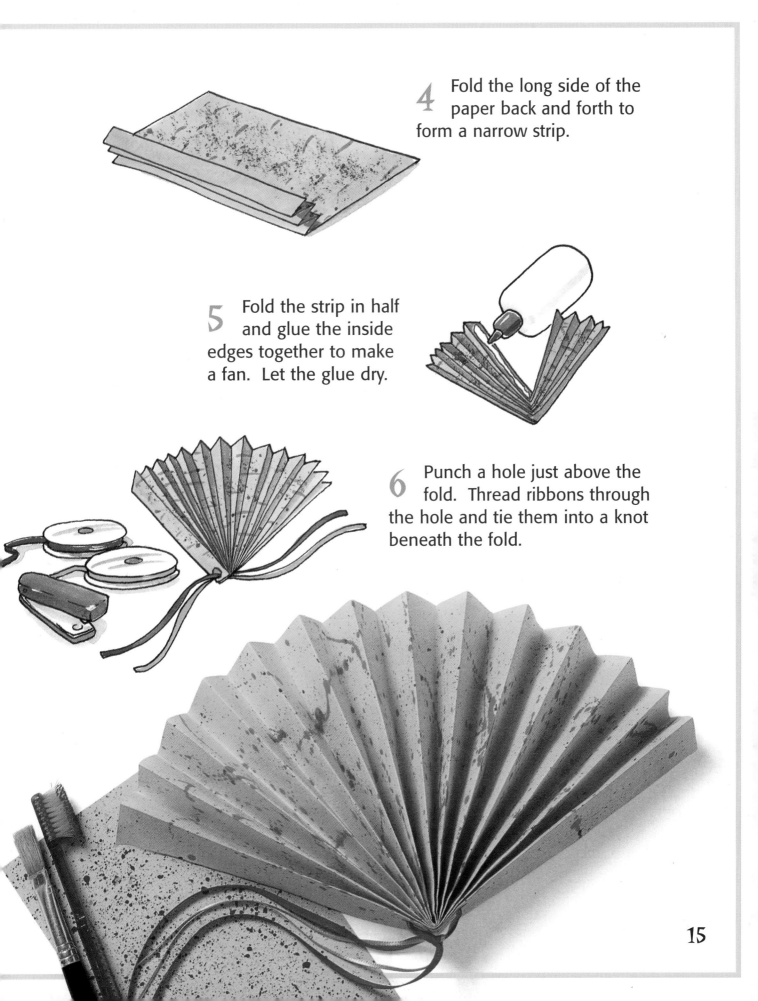

4 Fold the long side of the paper back and forth to form a narrow strip.

5 Fold the strip in half and glue the inside edges together to make a fan. Let the glue dry.

6 Punch a hole just above the fold. Thread ribbons through the hole and tie them into a knot beneath the fold.

Comb Creations

A cardboard comb with blunt teeth won't take the tangles out of your hair, but it can make eye-catching wave patterns in paste paint.

1 To make paste paint, mix equal amounts of flour and water in a bowl. Add a little paint and stir the mixture until it is smooth.

2 To make a comb with blunt teeth, cut a rectangle out of cardboard, then cut triangle-shaped notches along one short side of the rectangle.

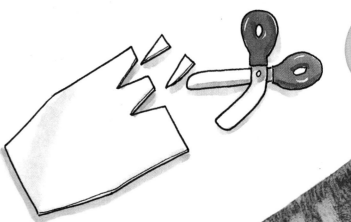

16

3 Brush paste paint over an entire sheet of thick paper. Use your cardboard comb to make wavy patterns in the paint. Wipe the paint off the comb each time you use it.

4 When the paint is dry, wrap the paper around a small box and glue or tape the ends to hold the paper in place. Cut a slot in the top of the box to make a coin bank.

★ **Helpful Hint** ★
Combed paper makes beautiful gift wrap.

Loose Marbles

Don't lose your marbles — you'll need them to paint this fantastic place mat.

1   Cut the front off a cereal box, then cut a sheet of white paper to fit the bottom of the box. Lay the paper inside the box.

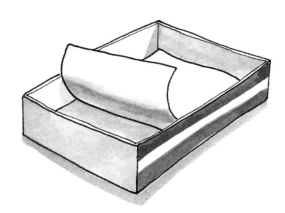

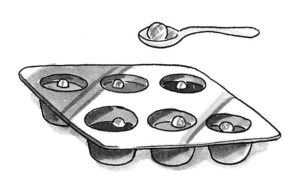

2   Put different colors of paint into the cups of a muffin pan. Drop a marble into each cup. Pick up each paint-coated marble with a spoon and drop the marble into the box.

3 Gently move the box so the marbles roll around, leaving paint trails. Wash the marbles before recoating them with paint.

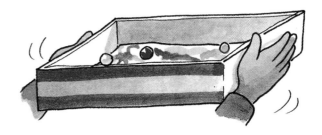

4 When the paint is dry, take the paper out of the box and lay it face down on clear adhesive-backed plastic. Cut out square pieces at the corners of the plastic. Fold the flaps over to stick them on the back of the place mat.

★ **Bright Idea** ★
Make a place mat for every member of the family.

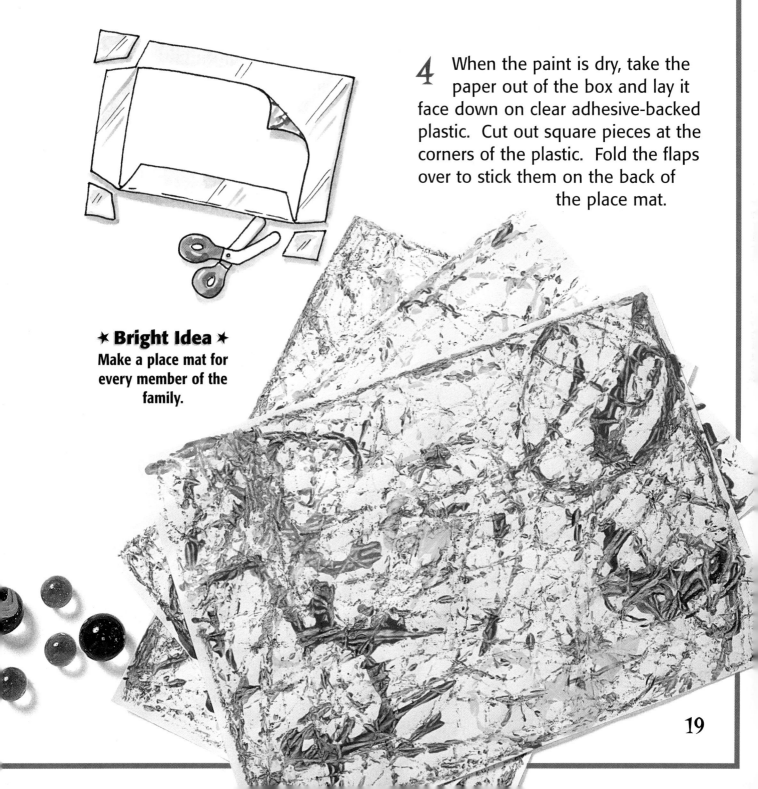

Nature's Stamps

Large leaves make pretty prints on pots for plants — or almost anyplace!

1   Make sure your flowerpot is clean. Then, with a flat paintbrush, paint the outside of the pot. Let the paint dry.

2   Paint evenly over one side of a leaf, but do not paint the leaf's stem.

★ **Bright Idea** ★
Put plants in your pots or use them to store odds and ends.

3 Lay the leaf, paint side down, on the pot. Place a piece of clean paper on top of the leaf and rub over it with your fingers. Remove the paper and the leaf. Repeat steps 2 and 3 to make more leaf prints.

4 With a pointed paintbrush, paint a stem for each leaf on the pot. Paint a pattern around the pot's rim, too. When the paint is dry, brush on a coat of varnish.

Prints Charming

You Will Need

- pencil
- felt
- scissors
- white glue
- cardboard
- clear tape
- flat paintbrush
- paint
- paper

Turn plain paper into amazing gift wrap almost faster than you can say "presto."

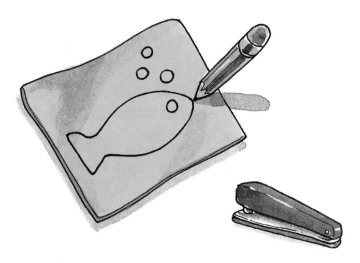

1 Draw simple shapes on a piece of felt and cut them out.

2 Glue the felt shapes onto a piece of cardboard. Fold a piece of tape (as shown) and stick it onto the back of the cardboard to make a handle.

3 Brush paint onto the felt shapes, making sure the paint covers them completely.

4 Hold the cardboard by the handle and press it, felt side down, firmly onto the paper. Then, lift it off and brush more paint onto the felt to make another print. Keep printing until the paper is covered with your prints.

Serious Stencils

**Stencil some stationery with
a snappy design — again and
again and again!**

1 Cut thin cardboard into
a small rectangle.

2 Draw a simple
shape on the
cardboard.

3 Ask an adult to cut out the
shape with a craft knife.
Now you have a stencil. Brush
varnish over the stencil, so the
stencil will last longer.

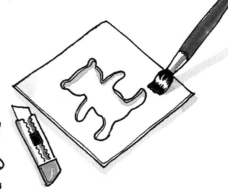

24

4 When the varnish is dry, place the stencil on a piece of stationery. Pour thick paint onto a saucer.

5 Dip a sponge into the paint and dab it lightly onto the stencil until the design is filled in.

★ **Bright Idea** ★
Stencil envelopes to match your stationery.

Crayon Crazy

You Will Need
- pencil and ruler
- cardboard
- photograph
- craft knife
- crayons
- thick black paint
- flat paintbrush
- clear tape

Your favorite photograph will look great in this fantastic frame.

1 Draw a rectangle that is slightly smaller than your photo in the center of a piece of cardboard. Ask an adult to cut out the rectangle with a craft knife.

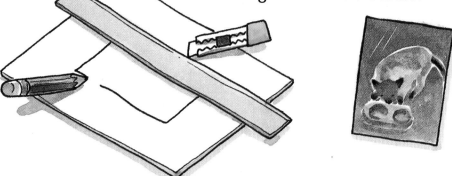

2 Now you have a frame. Color the front of the frame with crayons, changing colors as you go around the frame.

3 Paint over the crayon with thick black paint until the frame is completely covered with paint. Let the paint dry.

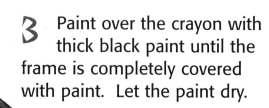

4 Use the end of the paintbrush to scratch a pattern in the paint. The crayon will show through.

5 Tape your photo onto the back of the frame. To make a stand, cut a triangle out of cardboard and tape it to the back of the photo.

★ **Bright Idea** ★
Try gluing your photo onto a background of colored paper.

27

Dare to Tear?

Put down the paintbrush and tear up the paper to see the amazing artwork you can make without paints and brushes.

1 Tear colored paper into strips and shapes. Arrange the torn pieces on white paper to create a picture.

2 Glue each piece of torn paper in place.

28

3 Use the edge of a ruler to tear four strips of cardboard. Arrange the strips around the sides of your picture to make a frame.

4 Glue the cardboard frame in place with the ends overlapping. Decorate the frame with more pieces of torn paper.

★ **Helpful Hint** ★
A glue stick works best for this project.

29

Ah-Tissue!

Scrunch tissue paper into rosebud-sized balls to decorate dainty butterflies for a fluttering mobile.

You Will Need
- black marker
- thin cardboard
- colored tissue paper
- white glue
- scrap paper
- scissors
- needle and thread
- wooden skewers

1 Use a black marker to draw four large butterflies on thin cardboard. Color in the bodies of the butterflies with the black marker, too.

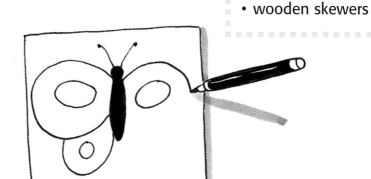

2 Tear tissue paper into small squares and scrunch each square into a ball. You will need a lot of tissue paper balls to fill each butterfly.

3 Pour some glue onto a piece of scrap paper. Dip a tissue paper ball into the glue, then stick it onto a butterfly. Fill all four butterflies with tissue paper balls.

4 Cut out each butterfly and use a needle and thread to poke a hole through the top. Pull the thread through the hole and tie the thread in a knot.

5 Glue two wooden skewers together to form a cross. Tie thread in the center of the cross to hang the mobile. Tie a butterfly onto the end of each skewer.

★ **Helpful Hint** ★
Adjust the thread to balance the mobile.

Cool Collage

The kitchen is a good place to find many odds and ends for creating a clever collage.

1 Collect odds and ends, such as noodles, toothpicks, and paper clips, from cupboards and drawers around the house. Ask for permission to use the items, then arrange them on a piece of cardboard.

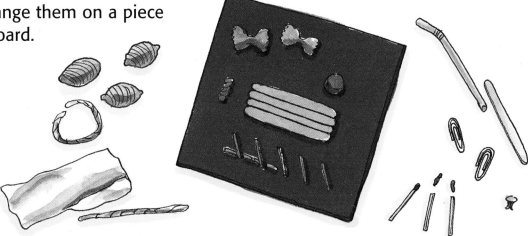

2 Take the items off the cardboard and paint them to make them more colorful.

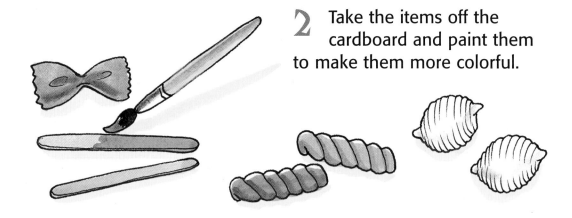

3 Let the paint dry, then glue the items in place on the cardboard.

4 Cut four strips of corrugated cardboard to fit around your collage. Cut the ends of the strips at an angle so the strips fit together neatly at each corner like a frame. Glue the strips onto the cardboard.

★ **Bright Idea** ★
Glue odds and ends onto a jar or a cookie tin to make decorative containers.

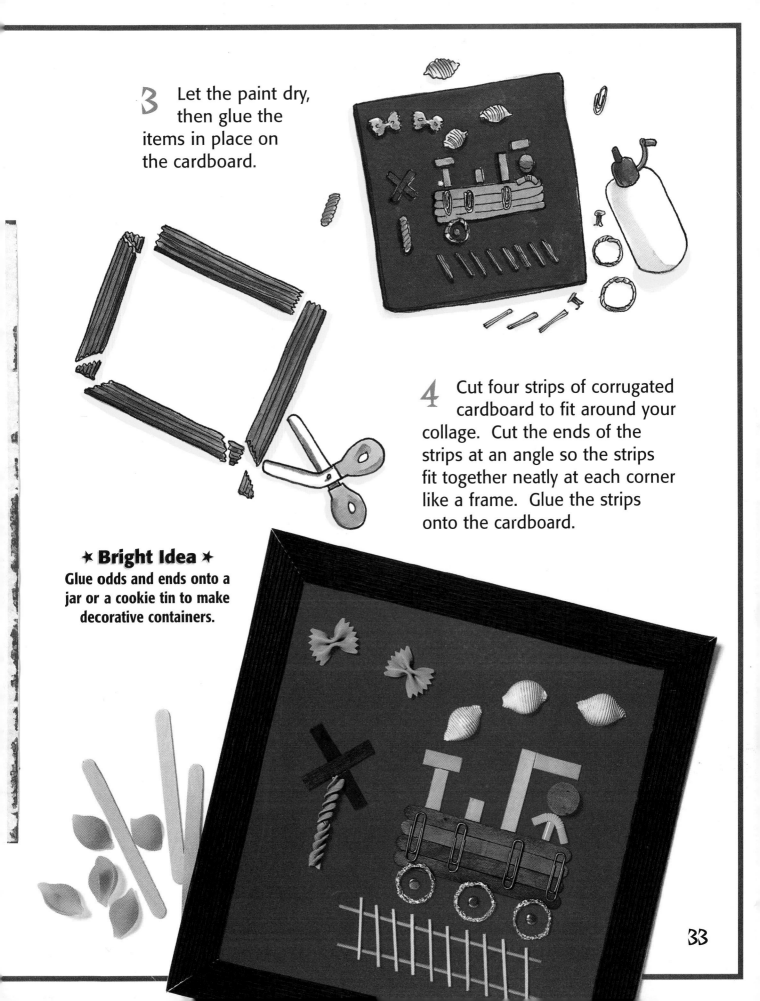

Bean Bonanza

Creating a mosaic takes patience, but it's lots of fun. Use beans and seeds of many different sizes and colors to make interesting designs.

You Will Need
- thin cardboard
- craft knife
- acrylic paint
- flat paintbrush
- pencil
- beans and seeds
- white glue
- clear varnish

1 Ask an adult to cut out a square piece of thin cardboard with a craft knife. Paint a base color on the cardboard.

2 When the paint is dry, draw a simple picture or pattern on the cardboard. Arrange beans and seeds of different sizes, colors, and shapes on different parts of the design.

3 Glue the beans and seeds in place. For small details, dip the bean or the seed in glue, then stick it in place.

4 To fill a large area, spread glue over the area, then sprinkle beans or seeds onto it and press them down with your fingers. When the design is filled in and the glue is dry, brush clear varnish over the entire mosaic.

★ **Helpful Hint** ★
Separate different kinds
of seeds and beans in the
cups of a muffin pan.

Why Dye?

Turn plain paper towels into stunning napkins that will make any meal more special.

You Will Need
- food coloring
- cups
- paper towels
- clothesline
- clothespins

1 Put several drops of food coloring into a cup. Use a separate cup for each color. Add a little water to each cup. The more water you add, the paler the colors will be.

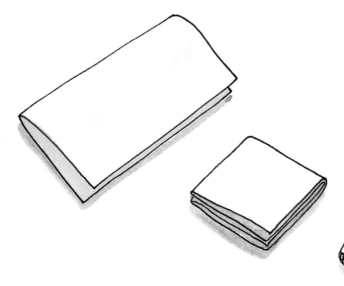

2 Fold a paper towel in half. Then fold it in half three more times to make a small square.

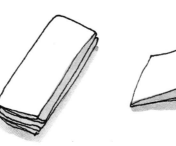

3 Dip each corner of
the folded paper
towel into a different
cup of colored water.

4 Carefully unfold the
paper towel and hang
it on a clothesline to dry.

★ **Helpful Hint** ★
Fold the paper towels all
different ways to make
unusual patterns.

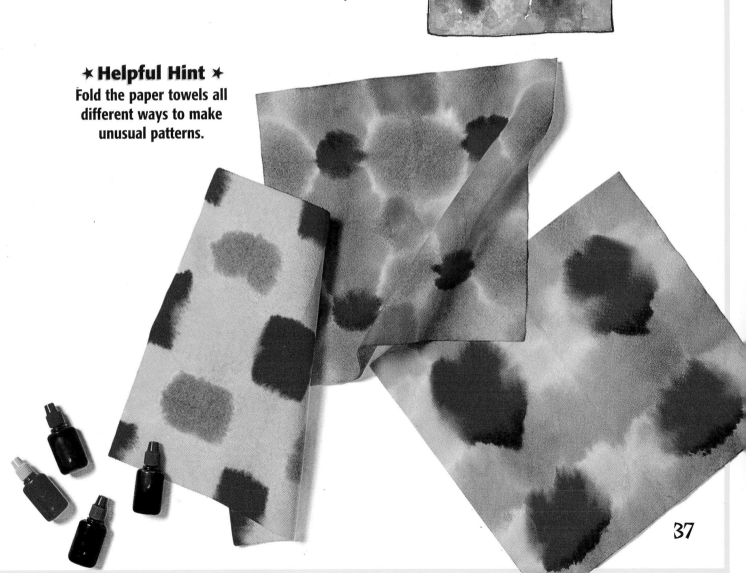

Marbling Magic

Capture swirling colors on paper to make magical designs.

1 Stir some nontoxic wallpaper paste into a pan of water until the mixture thickens.

2 Put different colors of paint into separate bowls and add water to thin them. Dip a straw into the paint and sprinkle the paint over the paste mixture. If the paint sinks, add more water to it.

3 Sprinkle different colors of paint onto the paste, then gently swirl the paints with a skewer.

4 Lay a piece of thick paper on the paste for about 15 seconds. Lift the paper off gently. The marbled paint should stay on the paper.

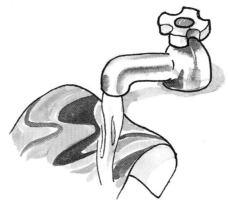

5 Rinse the marbled paper under cold running water. Lay it face up to dry.

6 Fold a piece of colored cardboard in half. Cut out a piece of the marbled paper and glue it to the colored cardboard to make a greeting card.

★ **Bright Idea** ★
Use marbled paper to make beautiful bookmarks and picture frames.

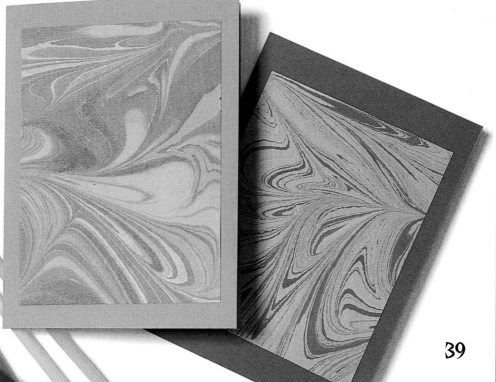

Fabulous Fabric

Fabric paints are fun!
Use them to cover a
T-shirt with hearts, hugs,
and kisses!

You Will Need
• T-shirt
• masking tape
• scissors
• cardboard
• fabric paints
• scrap paper

1 Tape a clean T-shirt onto your work area with masking tape.

2 Cut a piece of cardboard to fit inside the T-shirt. The cardboard will keep the shirt flat and stop paint from soaking through.

★ **Helpful Hint** ★
Ask an adult for help if
the paint needs to be set
by ironing it.

3 Shake fabric paints well before using them. Test each paint by practicing your design on scrap paper first.

4 Paint your T-shirt with dots, squiggles, and other designs. Be careful not to touch the paint while it is wet. Let the paint dry completely before you wear your new shirt.

41

Glass with Class

You Will Need
- glass jar
- small candle
- paint
- paintbrush
- modeling clay

A brightly painted glass jar makes a colorful candleholder. Its magical glow can make any evening extraordinary.

1 Choose a glass jar that is the right size for your candle. Wash and dry the jar and remove any labels.

2 Thin paint with water. Paint the bottom of the jar on the inside. Tilt the jar a little and turn it so the paint runs around the lower sides. Let the paint dry.

3 Holding the jar on its side, put the paintbrush inside the jar and drip another color of thinned paint next to the first one. Roll the jar slowly until the paint dries.

4 Continue dripping paint and rolling the jar until the entire inside of the jar is painted. Use a small ball of clay to attach the candle to the bottom of the jar. Ask an adult to light the candle.

★ **Bright Idea** ★
Put some candleholders on your dinner table to add an elegant touch.

43

Fantastic Plastic

Sunlight will dance through this colorful sun catcher to brighten your day.

You Will Need
- pencil
- paper
- tape
- sheet of acetate
- paintbrushes
- paint
- scissors

1   Draw a circle on a piece of paper. Draw a simple design inside the circle.

2   Tape a sheet of acetate over your drawing.

3   Fill in your design with thin paint and let the paint dry completely.

44

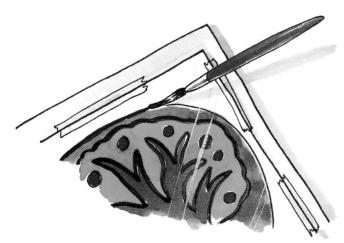

4 Paint the outline of the design and the circle around the design with black paint. Let the paint dry.

5 Cut out the acetate circle and tape it onto a window to let sunlight shine through it.

★ Helpful Hint ★
Use paints that are made for painting on glass.

Cut It Out!

Bright paint and paper shapes can turn a plain cookie tin into a work of art.

1 Make sure the cookie tin is clean and dry. Paint the sides and the lid with a coat of thick white paint. Let the paint dry.

2 Paint a bright color over the white paint. You might have to give the tin a second coat after the first coat dries.

3 Cut different shapes out of colored paper. Arrange the shapes to form a pattern or a picture.

4 Glue each shape onto the tin. Then brush a coat of clear varnish over the entire tin. Let the varnish dry.

★ **Bright Idea** ★
Decorate the sides of the cookie tin, too!

Glossary

acetate: clear, plasticlike material made of acid and cellulose, a substance found in plant cells.

base coat or **base color:** the first layer or color of paint put onto a surface.

blunt: not sharp; having a dull or a flat edge.

collage: artwork made by gluing a variety of objects onto a surface to form a creative pattern or design.

corrugated: having a surface with ridges and grooves in it.

marbled: streaked with colors in a pattern that looks like marble stone.

mosaic: artwork made by fitting small pieces of colored objects together to form a design.

nontoxic: not harmful or poisonous if swallowed or absorbed through the skin.

palette: a surface for mixing different colors of paint to create new colors.

spattering: scattering or sprinkling a liquid to make a spotted pattern.

skewers: pointed sticks used to hold meat together while the meat is roasting.

stationery: paper that is made for writing notes and letters.

stencil: a piece of stiff paper or cardboard with a design cut into it. When paint is spread over the stencil, the design is printed on the surface beneath it.

More Craft Books by Gareth Stevens

Animal Crafts. Worldwide Crafts (series).
Iain MacLeod-Brudenell

Crafty Stamping. Crafty Kids (series).
Petra Boase

Crafty T-Shirts. Crafty Kids (series).
Petra Boase

Kids Create! Williamson Kids Can!® (series).
Laurie Carlson

Index